Fun Fan Facts:
The Unofficial NBA Edition

San Antonio Spurs

Everything Young Spurs Fans Should Know

By: Jake Liam

Dedication

For every Spurs fan who was in the room when Ray Allen hit that shot and still hasn't fully recovered.

This one's for you. Go Spurs Go.

THE NBA BY THE NUMBERS

MOST NBA CHAMPIONSHIPS*

- CELTICS (18) [trophies] †
- LAKERS (17) [trophies]
- WARRIORS (7) [trophies]
- BULLS (6) [trophies]
- SPURS (5) [trophy]

As of the 2024-25 Season. † One Trophy = 4 Championships.

BIG NUMBERS

$156 million
Stephen Curry's est. earnings in the 24-25 season

7'7"
Tallest player in NBA history (Gheorghe Mureşan & Manute Bol)

NBA HISTORY SNAPSHOT

- **1946** NBA Founded
- **1954** Shot Clock Introduced
- **1979** 3-Point Line Added
- **2023** NBA Cup Introduced

30 | 4 | 82

30 Teams Competing in the NBA

4 Playoff Rounds

82 Games Per Season

SAN ANTONIO SPURS
IN THE NBA

- FOUNDED: 1976 †
- NBA TITLES: 5
- CONFERENCE TITLES: 6*

22 Consecutive Playoff Appearances

*† Founding dates are complicated & may cause arguments at Thanksgiving. Ask someone born before color TV. All Titles reflect pre-relocation franchise history. * As of 2024-25 Season.*

EASTERN CONFERENCE

- Atlantic – **Celtics**
- Atlantic – **Nets**
- Atlantic – **Knicks**
- Atlantic – **76ers**
- Atlantic – **Raptors**
- Central – **Bulls**
- Central – **Cavaliers**
- Central – **Pistons**
- Central – **Pacers**
- Central – **Bucks**
- Southeast – **Hawks**
- Southeast – **Hornets**
- Southeast – **Heat**
- Southeast – **Magic**
- Southeast – **Wizards**

WESTERN CONFERENCE

- Pacific – **Lakers**
- Pacific – **Clippers**
- Pacific – **Warriors**
- Pacific – **Suns**
- Pacific – **Kings**
- Northwest – **Nuggets**
- Northwest – **Timberwolves**
- Northwest – **Thunder**
- Northwest – **Trail Blazers**
- Northwest – **Jazz**
- Southwest – **Mavericks**
- Southwest – **Rockets**
- Southwest – **Spurs**
- Southwest – **Pelicans**
- Southwest – **Grizzlies**

NBA ALL-TIME MVP LEADERS

KAREEM ABDUL-JABBAR (6) ★ MICHAEL JORDAN (5) ★ BILL RUSSELL (5)

Introduction

Welcome, fans! Whether you're new to cheering for the San Antonio Spurs or you've been bleeding the team colors your whole life, this book is packed with fun, exciting facts about your favorite team. Get ready to impress your friends and family with everything you know about the Spurs.

Quick Time Out

This book is packed with stats. Like, A LOT of stats. Every fact was checked, double-checked, and triple-checked. But here's the thing about basketball history: not everyone agrees on everything. Ask someone who watched games before color TV and someone who grew up with instant replay and you'll get two completely different answers. My dad, stepdad, uncle, and grandpa all argued about the same fact. Four people. Four answers. All of them think they're right. So if you spot something that doesn't match what you've heard, congratulations. You might be a bigger fan than the people who helped make this book. And honestly? That's pretty cool.

HOW IT WORKS

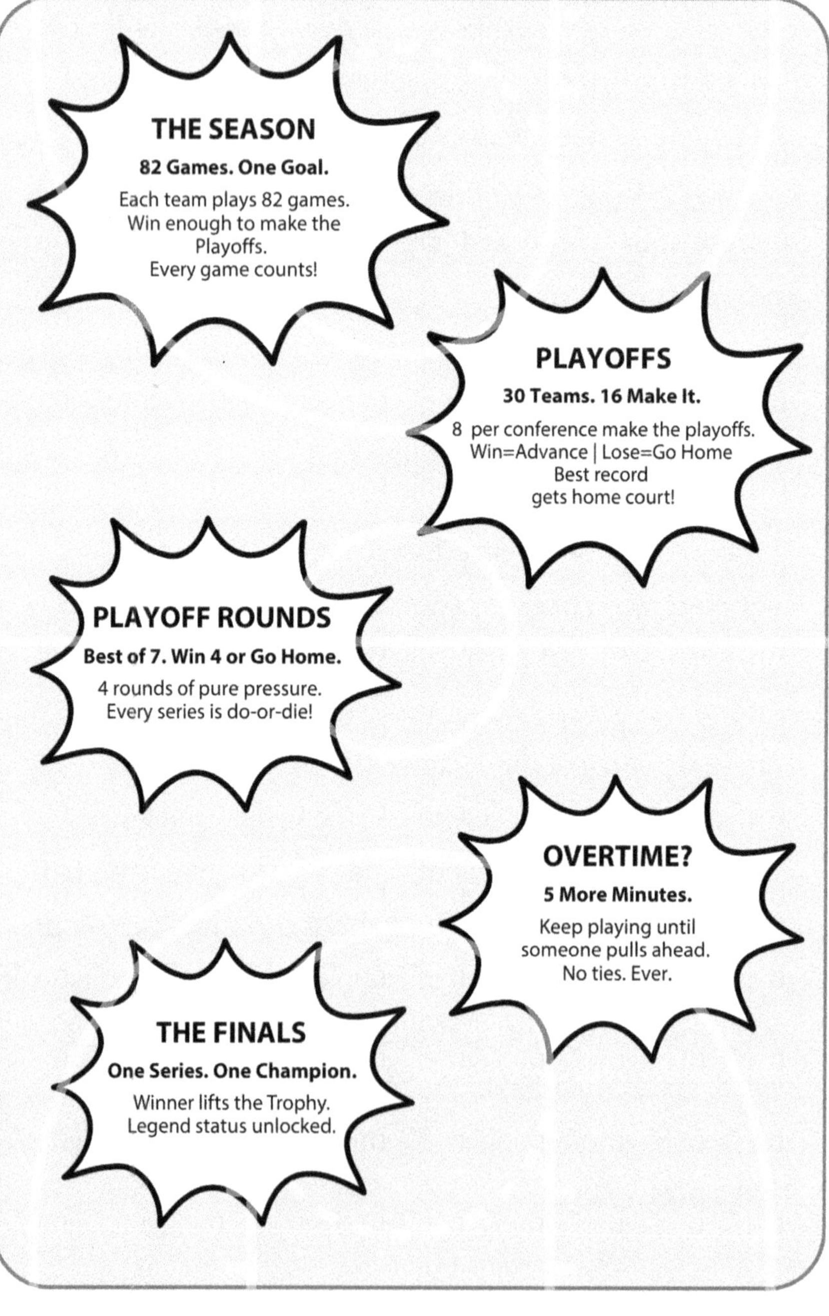

THE SEASON
82 Games. One Goal.
Each team plays 82 games.
Win enough to make the
Playoffs.
Every game counts!

PLAYOFFS
30 Teams. 16 Make It.
8 per conference make the playoffs.
Win=Advance | Lose=Go Home
Best record
gets home court!

PLAYOFF ROUNDS
Best of 7. Win 4 or Go Home.
4 rounds of pure pressure.
Every series is do-or-die!

OVERTIME?
5 More Minutes.
Keep playing until
someone pulls ahead.
No ties. Ever.

THE FINALS
One Series. One Champion.
Winner lifts the Trophy.
Legend status unlocked.

How the NBA Works

At first glance, basketball feels simple. Ten players. One ball. Two hoops. Go.

Then the NBA adds the layers.

An 82-game regular season. A draft where bad teams pick first. Playoffs that last two full months. Superstars who can change everything with one trade. Dynasties that rise, fall, and rise again.

And somehow, it all works.

The NBA is built on one big idea: every team gets a chance to reset, reload, and rise again. No relegation. No dropping down to a lower league. Just basketball, every night, from October through June.

It is a league designed for drama, stars, and comebacks. And once you understand the flow, it is impossible to stop watching.

The League Setup

The NBA has 30 teams, spread across the United States and Canada. Those teams are split into two conferences:

- Eastern Conference
- Western Conference

Each conference has three divisions, mostly based on geography. Divisions matter for scheduling, but not as much as they used to.

Every team plays 82 regular season games, usually from October through April. Home games. Road games. Back-to-back nights. Long road trips. The season is a marathon before the sprint even starts.

Win games, and you climb the standings. Lose too many, and the pressure builds fast.

How Games Are Played

An NBA game has four quarters, each lasting 12 minutes. That means 48 minutes of game time, plus timeouts, free throws, and the occasional coach argument that adds another 20 minutes nobody planned for.

Scoring is simple:

- A shot inside the three-point line is worth 2 points
- A shot beyond the arc is worth 3 points
- Free throws are worth 1 point

If the score is tied at the end of regulation, the game goes to overtime, which lasts 5 minutes. Still tied? Another overtime. Keep going until someone wins.

There is a shot clock too. Teams have 24 seconds to take a shot. No standing around. No holding the ball forever. Keep it moving.

The Regular Season Race

The regular season is long for a reason. It tests everything.

Depth. Health. Focus. Patience.

Teams play opponents from both conferences, but they face conference rivals more often. By the end of the season, each conference's top teams have earned their playoff spots the hard way.

The goal is simple: make the playoffs. But there is a twist.

The NBA Cup

In 2023, the NBA added something new to the middle of the season. Something with actual stakes. They called it the In-Season Tournament, now known as the NBA Cup.

It works like this: Every team plays a small group stage during November and December, with special court designs that look like nothing else in basketball. The best teams advance to a knockout round held in Las Vegas.

The winners split a prize pool. Players earn bonus money. And for the first time, a team could lift a trophy before the playoffs even started.

Some fans are still warming up to it. Some players love it. But the moment a team starts treating it seriously and a crowd shows up buzzing in December, it feels like something.

Which, honestly, sounds about right.

The Play-In Tournament

Instead of sending the top eight teams from each conference straight to the playoffs, the NBA added something new. The Play-In Tournament.

Here is how it works:

- Teams ranked 1 through 6 in each conference are safe
- Teams ranked 7 through 10 fight for the final two playoff spots

The 7 and 8 seeds have an advantage. Win once and you are in. Lose and you still get one more shot. The 9 and 10 seeds have to win twice in a row just to earn a first-round matchup.

It turns the end of the season into a sprint. Every game suddenly matters more. Fans love it. Coaches age rapidly.

The NBA Playoffs

Once the playoffs begin, everything tightens.

Sixteen teams enter. Eight from each conference. Every round is a best-of-seven games series. That means the first team to win four games moves on:

- First Round
- Conference Semifinals
- Conference Finals
- NBA Finals

Home-court advantage matters. Crowds get louder. Rotations get shorter. Superstars play heavier minutes. One bad quarter can flip a series. One great performance can define a career.

By the time the NBA Finals arrive in June, only two teams are left. One from the East. One from the West.

Four wins away from a championship. Four wins away from history.

The NBA Draft: Hope Begins Here

Here is where the NBA gets clever. Every summer, new players enter the league through the NBA Draft. Teams take turns selecting college players, international stars, and teenagers straight out of high school.

The teams that finished with the worst records get the best odds to pick early through the Draft Lottery. It is not guaranteed, but it gives struggling franchises a real shot at changing their future with one pick.

That means one bad season does not doom you forever. It might actually change everything. Some franchises are rebuilt by a single draft night moment.

Hope shows up wearing a new jersey.

No Relegation. All Pressure.

Unlike many global sports leagues, NBA teams never drop down to a lower league. They always stay in the NBA.

That does not mean there is no pressure.

Fans remember losing seasons. Owners make changes. Coaches get replaced. Players get traded. Every year is a test of direction, patience, and belief.

Stars, Systems, and Showtime

The NBA is famous for its stars. But stars do not win alone.

Teams need chemistry. Coaches need systems. Role players need to deliver on the biggest stages. One injury. One hot streak. One trade deadline deal. Any of it can flip a season.

That balance between individual brilliance and team basketball is what makes the league special.

Fast breaks. Buzzer-beaters. Game 7s. And moments that get replayed forever. That is the NBA.

Once you get the flow, it is pure electricity.

San Antonio Spurs Facts

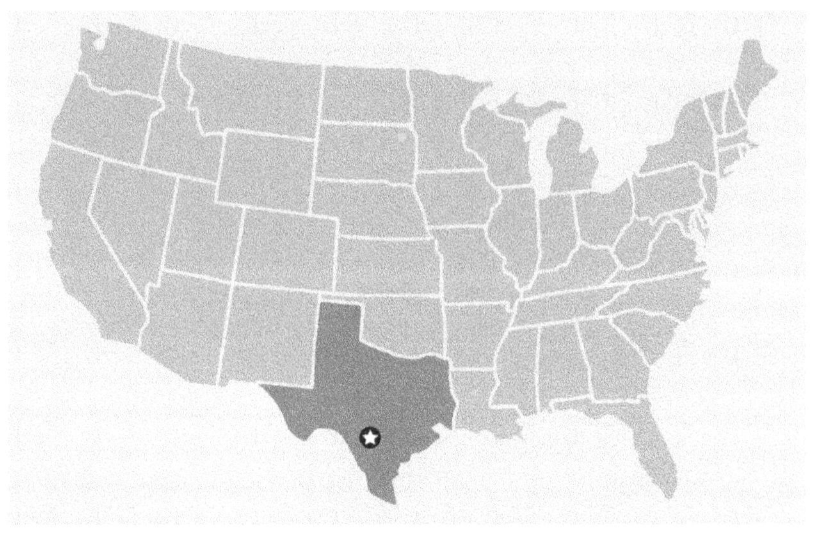

Home City

San Antonio, Texas

Home City Metro Area Population

about 2.6 million

Home Arena

Frost Bank Center

Max Capacity: 18,418

Famous Local Food

Breakfast tacos, puffy tacos, tamales, Tex-Mex, brisket

Conference / Division

Western / Southwest

Chapter 1: From Cowboy Town to Title Town

1. The Dallas Team Nobody Wanted

Picture a basketball team in Dallas that Dallas itself couldn't be bothered to show up for. That was the Dallas Chaparrals, a founding member of the American Basketball Association back in 1967. The ABA was the NBA's rival league and they played with a red, white, and blue ball that looked like it belonged at a birthday party. The Chaparrals had the ball. They just didn't have fans.

Attendance was so bad that in 1970 the team tried a desperate experiment. They renamed themselves the Texas Chaparrals and spread their home games across three cities, Dallas, Fort Worth, and Lubbock, hoping a wider regional approach would finally get people interested. It did not. Fort Worth got dropped after two months. Lubbock barely survived the season. The whole thing was abandoned after one year and the team quietly went back to being the Dallas Chaparrals, as if none of it had ever happened. Their final home game in Dallas drew exactly 134 paying customers. One hundred and thirty four people. For a professional basketball game. That is not a crowd. That is a birthday party.

A group of San Antonio businessmen bought the team in 1973, moved them south, renamed them the Spurs, and watched the city fall in love immediately. San Antonio adopted the Spurs the way you adopt a stray dog. Completely, immediately, and with zero intention of ever letting go.

2. Joining the Big League

In 1976 the NBA and the ABA agreed to merge. Four ABA teams got the golden ticket into the NBA: the Denver Nuggets, Indiana Pacers, New York Nets, and the San Antonio Spurs. The NBA made each team pay a fee just to walk through the door. It was basically a cover charge for the coolest party in sports.

The early NBA years were a learning curve. San Antonio wasn't winning championships yet. But they had something a lot of cities didn't. A fanbase that showed up regardless. They packed the arena, they were loud, and they were loyal. Nobody knew it yet, but this franchise was about to become one of the NBA's great stories. They were going to get a very large hint soon.

A very, very large hint.

3. The Admiral Reports for Duty

David Robinson was drafted by the Spurs in 1987 with the first overall pick. There was just one small scheduling conflict. He owed the United States Navy two more years of active service. So the Spurs drafted him, waved goodbye, and waited. For two whole years. They just sat there and waited for their franchise player to finish serving his country.

When Robinson finally arrived in 1989, he made the wait look extremely worth it. He was seven feet tall, could run like a guard, and had arms that seemed to go on about three extra inches longer than they should. In his very first season the Spurs improved by 35 wins. Thirty-five. That is not a typo. They went from a 21-win disaster to a 56-win contender because one single person finally showed up to work.

He earned the nickname The Admiral because of his Navy background and it fit perfectly. He commanded the paint, he commanded respect, and he was about to help build something massive. More on that in Chapter 2.

4. The Worst Season Money Can't Buy

Here is a sentence that should not make sense: the San Antonio Spurs once tried very hard to lose. On purpose. With enthusiasm.

The 1996-97 season was a beautiful disaster. David Robinson got injured early and missed almost the whole year. Without their anchor the Spurs collapsed to a 20-62 record, one of the worst in franchise history. At the end of the season they entered the NBA Draft Lottery with their eyes locked on one specific prize. A college junior from Wake Forest named Tim Duncan.

They won the lottery. They got the first pick, selected Tim Duncan, and essentially hit the cheat code for the next two decades of basketball. The most productive losing season in NBA history. San Antonio will never officially admit they were trying to lose and nobody can prove it. But the grin on the city's face in June 1997 said everything.

5. Pop Takes the Wheel

Gregg Popovich did something in November 1996 that very few people in any profession have ever done. He fired his own coach. As the team's General Manager, Pop decided mid-season that head coach Bob Hill wasn't the answer, removed him from the job, and appointed himself as the replacement. His own replacement. For his own decision.

It sounds like something a kid does in a video game when they're losing badly. But it worked. Pop installed a system built on defense, discipline, and the idea that basketball was supposed to look like a team sport. No hero ball. No ego. Everyone moves, everyone passes, everyone knows their role.

What followed was one of the greatest coaching runs in American sports history. Five championships. More wins than almost anyone who ever drew up a play on a whiteboard. It all started with Pop essentially giving himself a promotion during a losing streak. Honestly? Respect.

6. David Robinson (The Admiral, 1989-2003)

You already know how he got here. But think about what it actually meant to finally walk into that arena in 1989 after two years of military service, carrying the weight of an entire city's patience on your shoulders. No preseason. No warm-up lap. Just a gym full of people who had been waiting 730 days to see if you were worth it. Robinson laced up his sneakers and answered that question before Christmas.

Robinson won Rookie of the Year in his first season, which surprised nobody who watched him play and absolutely nobody who watched the Spurs win 35 more games than the year before. What followed was one of the most decorated individual careers in NBA history. A scoring title. A Defensive Player of the Year award. An MVP in 1995. Eleven All-Star selections. He was the kind of player who made every category on the stat sheet feel like a personal insult to whoever was guarding him.

For most of the early 1990s Robinson carried the Spurs as their sole reason for optimism, which is a heavy thing to ask of one person. He did it without complaint and without drama, which if you know anything about the Spurs should surprise you exactly zero percent. Then a skinny kid from Wake Forest arrived in 1997 and everything changed. Robinson did not sulk about sharing the spotlight. He embraced it completely, reinvented his role, and won two championships alongside Tim Duncan to close out his career.

His final game as a professional was a championship. He rode into the sunset on a parade float, two rings on his fingers and nothing left unfinished. The Admiral had left the court the only way a sailor should. With every flag flying.

7. Tim Duncan (The Big Fundamental, 1997-2016)

Tim Duncan played 19 seasons in the NBA, won five championships, made 15 All-Star teams, and finished as one of the five greatest players in the history of the sport. He did all of this while looking like a man standing in line at the post office. No expression. No celebration. No drama. He would hit a game-winning shot and his face would do absolutely nothing. Teammates would be losing their minds and Tim Duncan would look like he was thinking about what to have for lunch.

His nickname was The Big Fundamental because his game was built entirely on doing the basic things perfectly. The bank shot. The footwork. The positioning. While other players were throwing down monster dunks and pointing at the crowd, Duncan was quietly executing a textbook mid-range jumper off the glass for the nine hundredth time that season. It was not flashy. It was also completely unguardable for two decades.

He retired in 2016 at 40 years old, still good enough to play, and announced it with a single sentence on the Spurs website. No farewell tour. No documentary. No goodbye speech. Just Tim Duncan, clocking out, going home. Nineteen years, five rings, zero fuss. The most Tim Duncan ending imaginable.

Tim Duncan waits in the paint wearing #21 for the San Antonio Spurs. Calm face. No panic. Just the "Big Fundamental" ready to go to work. Duncan led the Spurs to their first championship in 1999 and eventually won five NBA titles, proving that quiet dominance can be just as scary as flashy highlights. *Photo: Tim Duncan in the paint vs the Milwaukee Bucks. Photograph via Wikimedia Commons. Licensed under CC BY-SA 2.0. Source: Wikimedia Commons.*

8. Tony Parker (TP, 2001-2018)

Tony Parker grew up in France, got drafted by a Texas basketball team at 19 years old, and within a few years became one of the best point guards in the NBA. His path to San Antonio began when he played in front of Spurs scouts at a pre-draft workout and was so good that they immediately called the office and told them to move up in the draft. He was picked 28th overall. Twenty-eighth. Seventeen teams passed on him twice. Those teams spent the rest of the decade watching him dismantle their defenses and feeling genuinely bad about their choices.

Parker was almost impossible to guard because of one extremely irritating habit. He would drive toward the basket at full speed, leap, and then somehow release the ball while floating sideways through the air at an angle that made no physical sense. Defenders called it the floater. Opponents called it other things that we cannot print in this book.

He won four championships with the Spurs and was named Finals MVP in 2007, becoming the first European player to ever win that award. A French teenager flew to Texas, learned the system, mastered the language, and then became the best player on the best team in basketball. If that is not a story worth knowing, nothing is.

9. Manu Ginobili (Manu, 2002-2018)

Manu Ginobili was the most chaotic good player in NBA history. Every single night he would do something that made you cover your eyes and then something else that made you completely forget about the first thing. He drove into traffic that no rational human being would drive into. He flung himself at the floor with zero concern for his own body. He threw passes that should not have worked and then they worked and nobody could explain why.

He didn't invent the Euro step, but he introduced it to NBA fans and made it famous. The Euro step is a move where a player driving to the basket takes a step in one direction and then immediately plants and steps in a completely different direction, leaving the defender stumbling in the wrong lane. It exists in basketball at every level now, from the NBA to rec leagues to twelve-year-olds in driveways. Manu did not technically invent it but he brought it to the NBA and made it famous, and every player who uses it today is running a move with a European accent because of him.

He also, at the peak of his career, went completely bald. Just fully committed. Shaved it all off and kept playing at an elite level, which sends a very encouraging message to everyone's fathers. Manu won four championships, an Olympic gold medal with Argentina, and the hearts of every Spurs fan who ever watched him throw his body into a situation that had no business ending well and somehow come out fine.

10. Kawhi Leonard (The Klaw, 2011-2018)

Kawhi Leonard has some of the largest hands ever measured at the NBA Draft Combine. Every year the top college players entering the NBA Draft get measured head to toe at the Draft Combine. Hand size, wingspan, vertical jump, all of it. Kawhi's hands were the biggest ever recorded there. Eleven and a half inches across. For context, a standard dinner plate is about ten and a half inches across. Kawhi Leonard can palm a dinner plate like it is a grape. When he catches a basketball it basically disappears. Defenders trying to poke the ball away from him have described the experience as attempting to steal something from a mechanical claw machine. Hence the nickname.

He was also one of the quietest superstars the league has ever seen. Not shy. Not unfriendly. Just very, very quiet. Teammates would describe practice as going great and Kawhi would nod and say nothing. Reporters would ask him questions and receive answers that were technically words but communicated almost nothing. He once laughed at a press conference and the clip went so viral that people are still watching it today because it sounded like a sound effect from a cartoon robot discovering joy for the first time.

On the court none of that mattered because Kawhi Leonard was a defensive force that made the best offensive players in the world visibly unhappy. He locked down LeBron James. He locked down Kevin Durant. He won two Defensive Player of the Year awards. He won the 2014 Finals MVP. Then he left San Antonio, broke Toronto's heart too, and ended up in Los Angeles. But that 2014 championship run belongs to the Spurs forever, and his giant hands were all over it.

Chapter 3: When San Antonio Stopped the World

11. The Lockout Championship Nobody Saw Coming

In 1998 the NBA had a labor dispute between the owners and players that shut down the entire season until February 1999. The schedule got chopped to 50 games. No training camp. No preseason. Just a rushed, chaotic, everyone-is-out-of-shape sprint to the playoffs. Most teams were a mess. The San Antonio Spurs were not most teams.

With Tim Duncan in his second year and David Robinson still patrolling the paint, the Spurs went 37-13 in the shortened season and then tore through the playoffs like they had been waiting in a room by themselves for months with nothing to do except get ready. Which, to be fair, they basically had. They swept the Los Angeles Lakers. They beat the Portland Trail Blazers. They took the Finals in five games against the New York Knicks, who had somehow snuck into the playoffs as the eighth seed and immediately regretted every decision that led them there.

Tim Duncan won Finals MVP. David Robinson finally got his championship ring after twelve years of being excellent without one. The whole thing took place during a season that almost did not happen, against a backdrop of chaos and complaints, and the Spurs handled it like it was a minor inconvenience. Their first championship arrived wearing a hard hat and a slightly shorter calendar. Nobody saw it coming. San Antonio did not care.

12. Four More and a Dynasty Is Born

Winning one championship is hard. Winning five over fifteen years while the entire league is specifically trying to stop you is something else entirely. That is what the San Antonio Spurs did between 1999 and 2014, and the truly annoying part for everyone else is how consistently they did it.

They won in 2003 behind Tim Duncan's complete destruction of the New Jersey Nets. They won in 2005 when they beat the Detroit Pistons in seven brutal games that contained approximately zero exciting plays but an enormous amount of excellent basketball. They won in 2007 by sweeping LeBron James's Cleveland Cavaliers so completely that LeBron left the court quickly after the loss, skipping the usual handshakes. Which tells you everything you need to know about how that felt from the other side. They won again in 2014, but that one gets its own story because it deserves it.

Five championships. Four different starting lineups. One coach. One system. Pop just kept swapping in players, explaining the rules, and winning. Other teams spent those fifteen years rebuilding, retooling, signing big free agents, and changing everything. The Spurs changed almost nothing. That was the point.

13. The Night Ray Allen Broke San Antonio's Heart

Imagine this. You are a Spurs fan. It is June 18, 2013. Game 6 of the NBA Finals. Your team leads the Miami Heat by five points with 28 seconds left. You are so close to a championship that you can practically feel the confetti. The arena is starting to tilt toward celebration. Someone somewhere in San Antonio is already getting the champagne out of the fridge.

Then everything falls apart in approximately eleven seconds.

The Heat hit a shot to cut it to three. The Spurs missed a free throw. A rebound bounced in the wrong direction. And then Ray Allen, standing in the corner, caught a pass and hit a three-pointer that tied the game with 5.2 seconds on the clock. The arena went silent in a way that arenas very rarely go silent. The Heat won in overtime and then won Game 7 two nights later. San Antonio had the trophy in their hands and dropped it. Spurs fans will tell you exactly where they were sitting when it happened. They will not tell you this happily. The good news is that the Spurs remembered too. They had plans.

14. The Most Beautiful Basketball Ever Played

The 2014 NBA Finals was the Spurs getting an entire year to think about what happened in Game 6 and then coming back and doing something about it in the most ruthlessly elegant way possible. They did not just beat the Miami Heat. They embarrassed them with kindness. They passed the ball so many times and so perfectly that defenders just started spinning in circles trying to figure out where it was going.

Game 3 was the moment everyone pointed at. The Spurs ran a possession where the ball touched every single player on the court before someone finally took an open shot. They finished with 25 assists on 34 made baskets. Basketball coaches still show that game to their players as an example of what the sport is supposed to look like when everyone stops being selfish and just moves the ball. It looked less like an NBA game and more like someone had programmed a video game on the maximum passing setting.

San Antonio won the series in five games. LeBron James, who had just beaten them the year before, later called that Spurs team the best he had ever played against. From LeBron James, that is not a compliment he hands out like candy. The Spurs took it, said very little, and went home to Texas.

15. The Shot That Should Not Have Counted

Sean Elliott was a small forward for the San Antonio Spurs who most casual fans could not have picked out of a lineup. He was not Tim Duncan. He was not David Robinson. He was the other guy, the quiet piece, the one who showed up and did his job without much fanfare. Then, a kidney transplant sidelined him in the 97-98 season, and his brother donated one of his own kidneys to give Sean his career back. There's a version of this story where Sean never sets foot on the court again. This is not that story.

On May 31, 1999, the San Antonio Spurs were playing the Portland Trail Blazers in Game 2 of the Western Conference Finals. The Spurs were down by one point with twelve seconds left. Sean Elliott caught a pass in the corner, planted both feet, and hit a three-pointer over the outstretched arm of Rasheed Wallace to give San Antonio the lead. They held on and won the game.

There was one small problem that replays immediately made very clear. Elliott's left heel was on the out of bounds line when he caught the ball. By every reasonable interpretation of the rules, the shot should not have counted. The referees let it stand. Portland was furious. San Antonio was delighted. The shot became known as the Memorial Day Miracle and is one of the most famous moments in Spurs history, celebrated for decades by a fanbase that has never once felt the need to bring up the heel.

Sean came back from losing a kidney, hit a shot that probably should not have counted, and helped launch the Spurs toward their first championship. The heel was on the line. The moment was not. Some things you just let go.

16. The Coyote Who Has Been Here Forever

The San Antonio Spurs mascot is a coyote named The Coyote, which is either the most confident naming decision in sports history or evidence that nobody in the room had any other ideas. There was no vote. No fan contest. No dramatic unveiling with a name like "Spur-nado" or "Sir Dunks-a-Lot." Just a coyote. Named The Coyote. Standing there.

He has been the Spurs mascot since 1983, which makes him one of the longest-running mascots in the NBA. Over four decades of performing at games, getting launched out of cannons, riding tiny motorcycles, and doing things that a full-grown adult in a furry suit should not be able to do athletically. The Coyote has outlasted entire rosters. He was there before Tim Duncan arrived. He was there when Duncan retired. He will probably still be there when everyone reading this book has their own kids.

The truly remarkable thing is that he does not have a more interesting name and nobody has ever successfully changed it. Forty years of championships, legends, and cultural moments, and the mascot is still just The Coyote. At this point it is not a name. It is a statement.

17. The Fiesta Colors That Broke the Internet Before the Internet Existed

In 1999, right in the middle of their first championship run, the San Antonio Spurs introduced alternate uniforms that looked like a pinata had exploded onto a basketball jersey. Turquoise. Orange. Green. Pink. Colors that had absolutely no business being on an NBA uniform worn by a team whose entire identity was built on discipline and restraint. Tim Duncan wore them. He did not look pleased.

The jerseys were called the Fiesta Colors, inspired by the famous Fiesta San Antonio celebration that takes over the city every April. San Antonio is a city that genuinely loves color and noise and celebration, and someone in the uniform department decided that the basketball team should reflect that. Loudly. The reaction from fans was mixed in the way that a fire alarm is mixed. Some people loved them immediately. Some people needed several years and a lot of distance before they came around.

They became collector's items. Then they became beloved. The Spurs brought them back as alternates years later and fans lost their minds in the best possible way. The same jerseys that looked like a mistake in 1999 became the most celebrated alternate uniforms in franchise history. Fashion is a long game and San Antonio eventually won it.

18. The Spurs Way

Every NBA team has a philosophy. Most of those philosophies involve finding the biggest, most talented players available and hoping they figure it out. The San Antonio Spurs had a different idea. Move the ball. Play defense. Know your role. Trust the system. Do not, under any circumstances, do anything that draws attention to yourself at the expense of the team.

It sounds simple. It is extremely not simple. The reason it sounds simple is because the Spurs made it look simple for twenty years, which is the most deceptive thing they ever did. Players would arrive in San Antonio having spent their entire careers as focal points and scoring options and suddenly they were running a specific play, in a specific spot, for a specific purpose, and if they did it right nobody would even notice them. That was the goal. Be invisible and excellent.

Players who bought in won championships. Players who did not buy in were traded quietly and efficiently before anyone had time to write a dramatic story about it. The Spurs Way was not a motivational poster. It was a standard. You either met it or you played somewhere else.

19. Gregg Popovich, Human Being

Gregg Popovich is the winningest coach in NBA history. He is also famously the most difficult interview in NBA history, which is an achievement that requires real commitment. Television reporters would approach him during games for a quick sideline chat and Pop would answer their questions in a way that was technically cooperative but made it extremely clear he would rather be doing literally anything else. One word answers. Long pauses. The occasional look that suggested he was questioning every decision that had brought both of them to this moment.

He is also deeply funny, fiercely loyal, and the kind of coach who genuinely cares about his players as human beings rather than basketball assets. He requires them to know world history. He takes the team to local restaurants in every city and makes them order things they have never tried. He gives speeches about empathy and leadership and paying attention to the world outside the gym. Some players found this unexpected. All of them respected it.

He has coached the Spurs since 1996 and has never won fewer than 37 games in a full 82-game season. Through five championship runs, dozens of roster changes, and thirty years of sideline press conferences he clearly did not enjoy, Pop has remained the same. Demanding, hilarious, occasionally terrifying, and absolutely correct about basketball almost all of the time. The reporters never stopped asking. He never started answering properly. It was its own kind of dynasty.

20. The Smallest Big City in Basketball

San Antonio is the seventh largest city in the United States. Most people forget this. Most people picture Texas cities and think Houston or Dallas first, and San Antonio just sits there being enormous while nobody gives it the credit it deserves. It has a population of about 1.5 million people inside the city limits alone. That is not a small town by any measurement available.

The Spurs have called three different arenas home over the years. They started at the old HemisFair Arena, which was famously one of the loudest buildings in the league. Then they moved to the Alamodome in 1993, which was a football-sized stadium that held 35,000 people and felt roughly as intimate as standing inside an airport hangar. Players hated the sight lines. Fans hated the cavernous echo. Everyone agreed it was enormous and wrong. In 2002 the Spurs finally got what they actually needed, a real basketball arena. The Frost Bank Center seats just over 18,000 people and every single one of them sounds like three. There is also a rodeo held there every February, which forces the entire Spurs team to pack their bags and go on an extended road trip while cattle take over the building. No other team in the NBA loses its home court to livestock. San Antonio would not have it any other way.

Other cities have spent decades trying to manufacture the relationship that San Antonio has with its team. You cannot manufacture it. You either have a city that genuinely loves its team or you do not, and San Antonio genuinely loves its team in a way that is almost inconvenient for everyone else trying to compete for attention. Seventh largest city in America. First in the hearts of Spurs fans everywhere. The math works fine.

Chapter 5: The Alien Has Landed

21. Life After the Big Three

When Tim Duncan retired in 2016 after nineteen seasons, the San Antonio Spurs did the reasonable thing and kept winning. They made the playoffs the next two seasons. They won 47 games and 48 games. They did not tank. They did not rebuild dramatically. They just quietly continued being competent while the rest of the league waited for them to fall apart.

Then Kawhi Leonard's relationship with the organization deteriorated in 2017 after a serious quad injury and a very long and public disagreement about his recovery timeline. The details were messy and both sides handled it in ways that made excellent newspaper copy. He was traded to Toronto in 2018 in a deal that brought back DeMar DeRozan, a beloved player who was himself surprised to find out he had been traded by text message. That is a whole other story.

What followed were a few years of genuine searching for identity. Good players, competitive seasons, first and second round playoff exits. The Spurs were no longer dynastically excellent but they were still professionally solid, which for most franchises is a perfectly acceptable outcome and for San Antonio felt faintly strange. They were used to more. They were about to get something they had never experienced before. Something seven feet four inches tall that moves like it was designed in a laboratory.

22. Victor Wembanyama: The Part Where Everyone Lost Their Mind

Before Victor Wembanyama was drafted first overall by the San Antonio Spurs in 2023, NBA scouts and executives and coaches and former players spent approximately two years publicly struggling to find the right words to describe what they were looking at. This is a group of professionals who get paid to evaluate basketball talent and have seen everything. They had not seen this.

He was seven feet four inches tall with a wingspan of eight feet. His arms are so long that if he stood in your kitchen and spread them out he would touch both walls in most standard kitchens. He shot threes like a guard. He blocked shots like a player a foot shorter than him would never even attempt to block. He moved at a pace that made no sense for his size. One scout compared him to a player from another planet. The phrase alien started appearing in press coverage. It stuck immediately because nobody had a better word and alien was genuinely more accurate than anything else available.

The Spurs won the draft lottery and selected him, which meant San Antonio got to do something it had done before with David Robinson and Tim Duncan. Find an extraordinary player, hand him the keys, and watch what happens next. Twice that had ended in championships. The city held its breath.

23. Things Wembanyama Can Do That Make No Physical Sense

Victor Wembanyama can stand flat-footed and look over the top of most NBA point guards. He can also pick up the basketball with one hand the way you pick up an orange. His shooting release point is so high that traditional shot-blocking is not really an option against him. Players who have spent their entire careers developing the timing to challenge shots at the rim are suddenly eight inches too short to reach the ball when he releases it. The geometry just does not work in their favor.

He also blocks shots going backward. This sounds like it should be impossible. It is not. He has a combination of wingspan and instinct and coordination that allows him to contest shots while moving in the wrong direction, which means that even when defenders think they have gotten past him they discover they have not actually gotten past him. This is deeply annoying for everyone who is not a Spurs fan.

In his rookie season he averaged over 21 points, 10 rebounds, and 3.6 blocks per game. He became only the second player in NBA history to average those numbers in a single season. The first was Kareem Abdul-Jabbar, who is on the short list of greatest players in the history of the sport. Victor Wembanyama did it as a teenager. His second and third seasons have only added to the argument that something genuinely new is happening in San Antonio and the rest of the league is going to be dealing with it for a very long time.

24. Pop's Coaching Tree Takes Over the World

One of the stranger subplots of the Gregg Popovich era is what happened to all the assistants he trained. They left San Antonio, became head coaches elsewhere, and then kept winning. Mike Budenholzer won a championship with the Milwaukee Bucks. Brett Brown coached the Philadelphia 76ers. Ime Udoka coached the Boston Celtics to the Finals. Becky Hammon became one of the most respected coaches in women's basketball. Mike Brown became Coach of the Year with the Sacramento Kings.

It is like Pop runs a coaching school that disguises itself as an NBA organization. Assistants arrive, learn the system, absorb the culture, get promoted somewhere else, and immediately start competing for the best record in their conference. The Spurs have produced more successful head coaches than almost any franchise in professional sports, which is either a tribute to how good Pop is at developing talent or evidence that he is extremely hard to work for and people keep leaving to escape him. Almost certainly both.

What it means is that the Spurs Way did not stay in San Antonio. It spread. The emphasis on ball movement, defensive discipline, and treating players like intelligent adults who can learn a system spread across the league through all these assistants carrying it with them to new cities. Pop coached for decades and in doing so accidentally coached the whole league.

25. The Future Is Seven Feet Four Inches Tall

Here is where the San Antonio Spurs currently sit. They have the most exciting young player in basketball, a coach who has won five championships and shows no signs of retiring gracefully, a fanbase that has been through five title runs and knows exactly what sustained excellence looks like, and a city that has never once considered rooting for anyone else.

The Spurs are not the finished product right now. They are the version of the movie where the hero is still figuring things out but you can already see exactly how powerful they are going to be when everything clicks. Wembanyama is getting better every single season. The supporting cast is growing around him. Pop is still drawing up plays that make opponents feel like they studied the wrong exam.

Other franchises will spend the next decade trying to figure out how to build around a generational talent. San Antonio has done it twice before and both times ended with a parade. The confetti is stored somewhere in Texas, waiting patiently. The Coyote is stretching. And somewhere in the Frost Bank Center, a seven-foot-four basketball player with arms that should not be legal is putting up shots that nobody alive can contest. The next chapter of San Antonio Spurs basketball is already being written. It is going to be very, very tall.

Bonus Trivia Quiz!

You think you are a true Spurs fan? Try this bonus quiz!

1. What was the original name of the team before they became the San Antonio Spurs?

A) The San Antonio Stars
B) The Dallas Chaparrals
C) The Texas Cowboys
D) The Houston Rockets

2. Which rival league did the Spurs come from before joining the NBA?

A) The World Basketball Association
B) The Continental Basketball Association
C) The American Basketball Association
D) The National Basketball League

3. How many wins did the Spurs gain in David Robinson's very first season?

A) 20
B) 25
C) 30
D) 35

4. What job did David Robinson have before joining the Spurs?

A) College professor
B) United States Navy officer
C) High school basketball coach
D) Marine Corps drill sergeant

5. How did Gregg Popovich become the Spurs head coach in 1996?

A) He was hired after a national coaching search
B) He was promoted from assistant coach
C) He fired the previous coach and appointed himself
D) He won the job in a competition against other candidates

6. What was special about the 1998-99 NBA season when the Spurs won their first championship?

A) It was played entirely on neutral courts
B) The season was shortened to 50 games due to a labor dispute
C) It was the first season with a three-point line
D) Tim Duncan was injured for half the season

7. What is Tim Duncan's nickname?

A) The Tower
B) The Silent Assassin
C) The Big Fundamental
D) The Cornerstone

8. Tony Parker was picked 28th overall in the 2001 NBA Draft. Where is he from?

A) Spain
B) Germany
C) France
D) Belgium

9. What move did Manu Ginobili help make famous in the NBA?

A) The spin move
B) The Euro step
C) The step-back three
D) The reverse layup

10. What physical feature made Kawhi Leonard nearly impossible to guard one-on-one?

A) His jumping ability
B) His top-end speed
C) His enormous hands
D) His left-handed shooting

11. What are the Spurs' famous alternate uniforms inspired by?

A) The Texas state flag
B) The San Antonio River Walk
C) The Fiesta San Antonio celebration
D) The colors of the Alamo

12. What happened with 5.2 seconds left in Game 6 of the 2013 NBA Finals?

A) Tim Duncan missed two free throws
B) Ray Allen hit a corner three to tie the game
C) LeBron James dunked over two defenders
D) Manu Ginobili turned the ball over

13. What is the name of the Spurs' mascot?

A) Spur
B) Silver
C) The Coyote
D) Tex

14. How many NBA Championships have the San Antonio Spurs won?

A) Three
B) Four
C) Five
D) Six

15. How tall is Victor Wembanyama?

A) Seven feet one inch

B) Seven feet two inches

C) Seven feet three inches

D) Seven feet four inches

Super Fan Secret Challenge

Only a true Spurs fan will know this.

(No Answer Provided)

The San Antonio Spurs have one of the most famous moments in NBA Finals history. In Game 6 of the 2013 NBA Finals, a Spurs player missed a shot late in the game that could have clinched the championship. The ball bounced off the rim and chaos followed. Who took that shot, and how many seconds were left on the game clock when it went up?

A) Tim Duncan, 4.2 seconds

B) Manu Ginobili, 3.6 seconds

C) Tony Parker, 5.1 seconds

D) Kawhi Leonard, 2.7 seconds

Answer Key

1. B) The Dallas Chaparrals

2. C) The American Basketball Association

3. D) 35

4. B) United States Navy officer

5. C) He fired the previous coach and appointed himself

6. B) The season was shortened to 50 games due to a labor dispute

7. C) The Big Fundamental

8. C) France

9. B) The Euro step

10. C) His enormous hands

11. C) The Fiesta San Antonio celebration

12. B) Ray Allen hit a corner three to tie the game

13. C) The Coyote

14. C) Five

15. D) Seven feet four inches

NBA PLAYOFF BRACKET

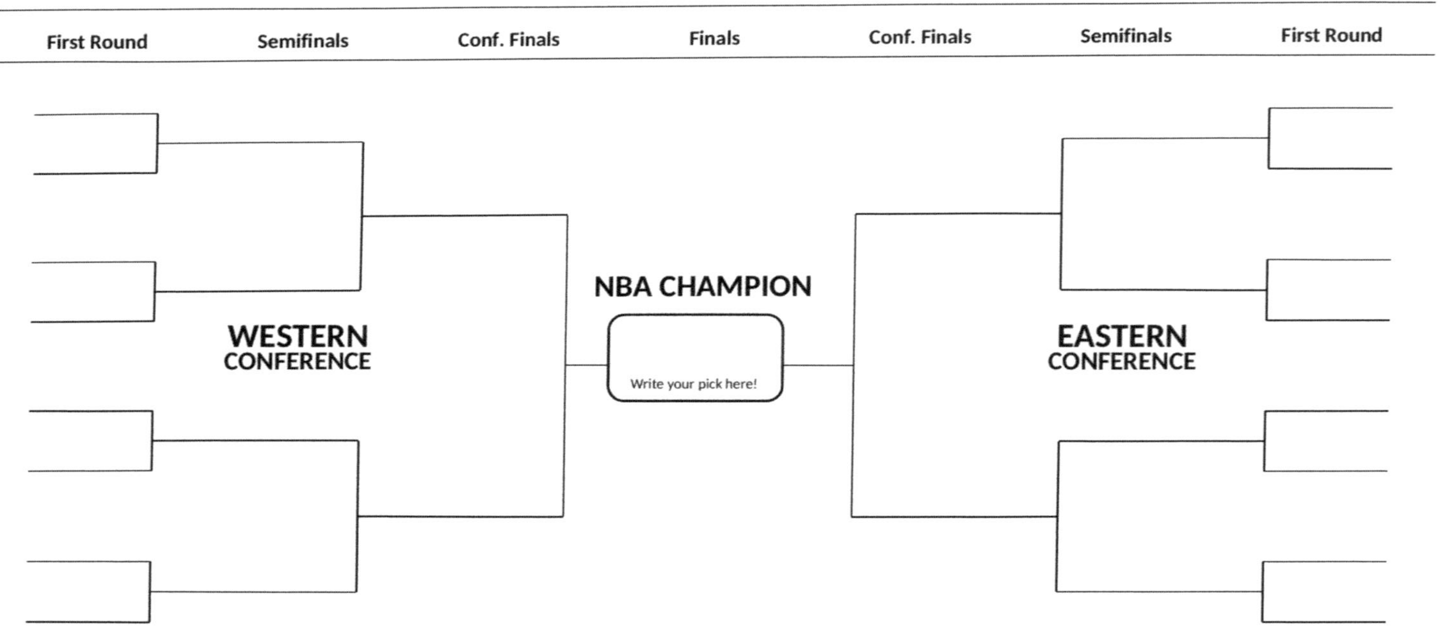

* Fill in your picks and try not to argue with your friends about it!

Part of the Fun Fan Facts: The Unofficial Sports Guide Series

Be the Boss of the Playoffs

You've broken down the matchups. You know which superstar takes over in the fourth quarter. You've seen the bench units that quietly decide series. You've watched the adjustments coaches make when their backs are against the wall.

Now it's time to stop watching and start deciding.

On this page, you are not just a fan. You are the Head Coach drawing up the last play with three seconds left on the clock. You are the GM who built this roster. You are the analyst who saw it all coming.

This is not just filling out a bracket.

This is building your championship run.

Sixteen teams enter the NBA Playoffs. The path is brutal. Best of seven. No shortcuts. No hiding. Every round gets louder, harder, and more personal.

This bracket is your Playoff Control Room.

The Game Plan

1. Survive Round One: Start with the opening round. Which matchup is going seven games? Who has the closer? Who folds under pressure? Make the calls.

2. Feel the Momentum: As you move into the Conference Semifinals and Conference Finals, things change. Role players become heroes. Stars feel the weight. Trust your reads.

3. Own the Finals: Trace your picks all the way to the NBA Finals. When the confetti falls and the trophy is raised, you'll find out who earned it.

House Rules: Circle your boldest upset. That is your official "I knew it" moment.

Choose Your Weapon: Pencil if you want flexibility. Pen if you trust your instincts. Sharpie if you believe in chaos.

Because once the playoffs tip off, there is no rewinding Game 7.

Make your picks. Trust your basketball brain. And let the playoff drama begin.

Fun Facts Wrap-Up

You made it through! You're officially a true superfan! Now it's time to put your knowledge to the test. Share these facts with friends and see who really knows their team best.

Love the series?

Your reviews help other fans discover Fun Fan Facts. If you enjoyed this book, we'd really appreciate you sharing your thoughts and leaving a review.

Want more Fun Fan Facts?

Scan the QR code below to visit our site and explore bonus trivia, challenges, and special extras - including new teams, future series, and collectible fun as they're released.

Collect All the Fun Fan Facts Series!

Check off every book you read. See the full set on Amazon. Search "Fun Fan Facts Jake Liam."

World Cup 2026 Edition

☐ Algeria
☐ Argentina
☐ Australia
☐ Austria
☐ Belgium
☐ Brazil
☐ Canada
☐ Cape Verde
☐ Colombia
☐ Croatia
☐ Curaçao
☐ Ecuador
☐ Egypt
☐ England

☐ France
☐ Germany
☐ Ghana
☐ Haiti
☐ Iran
☐ Ivory Coast
☐ Japan
☐ Jordan
☐ Mexico
☐ Morocco
☐ Netherlands
☐ New Zealand
☐ Norway
☐ Panama

☐ Paraguay
☐ Portugal
☐ Qatar
☐ Saudi Arabia
☐ Scotland
☐ Senegal
☐ South Africa
☐ South Korea
☐ Spain
☐ Switzerland
☐ Tunisia
☐ United States
☐ Uruguay
☐ Uzbekistan

World Cup 2026 Group Edition

☐ Group A
☐ Group B
☐ Group C
☐ Group D

☐ Group E
☐ Group F
☐ Group G
☐ Group H

☐ Group I
☐ Group J
☐ Group K
☐ Group L

English Football Edition

☐ Arsenal F.C.

☐ Aston Villa F.C.

☐ Chelsea F.C.

☐ Everton F.C.

☐ Fulham F.C.

☐ Liverpool F.C.

☐ Manchester City

☐ Manchester United

☐ Newcastle United F.C.

☐ Tottenham Hotspur

☐ West Ham United

☐ Wrexham A.F.C.

NBA Edition

☐ Atlanta Hawks

☐ Boston Celtics

☐ Brooklyn Nets

☐ Charlotte Hornets

☐ Chicago Bulls

☐ Cleveland Cavaliers

☐ Dallas Mavericks

☐ Denver Nuggets

☐ Detroit Pistons

☐ Golden State Warriors

☐ Houston Rockets

☐ Indiana Pacers

☐ LA Clippers

☐ Los Angeles Lakers

☐ Memphis Grizzlies

☐ Miami Heat

☐ Milwaukee Bucks

☐ Minnesota Timberwolves

☐ New Orleans Pelicans

☐ New York Knicks

☐ Oklahoma City Thunder

☐ Orlando Magic

☐ Philadelphia 76ers

☐ Phoenix Suns

☐ Portland Trail Blazers

☐ Sacramento Kings

☐ San Antonio Spurs

☐ Toronto Raptors

☐ Utah Jazz

☐ Washington Wizards

About the Author

Jake is a 13-year-old sports fan who loves football, American football, and basketball. He plays soccer as a goalie and dreams of one day playing for West Ham United and helping teach kids to love the game. His passion for sports runs in the family - his dad was a professional baseball player, and his stepdad sparked his love for West Ham. Through the Fun Fan Facts series, he shares the fun and excitement of sports with fans everywhere.

9 781972 300299